To: Kay,

MERELY MOVING
SHADOWS
Psalms 39:4-7 NLT

A 10-Week Devotional Guide to Living God's Purpose Through His Plan

Katie Stam Irk

Miss America 2009

miss America 2009

Esther Press Publishing
www.estherpress.com

Scripture quotations are taken from the *Holy Bible, New Living Translation*, copyright © 1996, 2004, 2007, 2013 by Tyndale House Foundation. Used by permission of Tyndale House Publishers, Inc., Carol Stream, Illinois 60188. All rights reserved.

Softcover ISBN-13: 978-0-9998545-0-1

10 9 8 7 6 5 4 3 2 1

For Brian, Charlotte, Rose, and Cubby.

Merely Moving Shadows

TABLE OF CONTENTS

Merely Moving Shadows

INTRODUCTION

"'Lord, remind me how brief my time on earth will be. Remind me that my days are numbered – how fleeting my life is. You have made my life no longer than the width of my hand. My entire lifetime is just a moment to you; at best, each of us is but a breath.' We are merely moving shadows, and all our busy rushing ends in nothing. We heap up wealth, not knowing who will spend it. And so, Lord, where do I put my hope? My only hope is in you." (Psalms 39:4-7, New Living Translation)

Yesterday is gone. Tomorrow is not promised. How do I make the most of today?

As we travel through life, we enter many different seasons. Leaving home, changing careers, getting married, experiencing parenthood, becoming an empty-nester, or entering into retirement each are times when we feel a major directional shift in our lives. It is in these seasonal transitions that we become the most reflective. We wonder if we're headed in the right direction, if we're walking the right path, and if we're abiding by God's will.

I don't want to be just a merely moving shadow. Busy rushing? Attempting to heap up wealth? Sounds pretty familiar. Instead, I want to lead a life that is fulfilling, meaningful, and leaves a legacy. We can do that by living a life based on biblical principles.

As a child, I saw the Bible as a collection of stories, miracles, and characters who did some really powerful things a really long time ago. The older I have become, the more I view scripture as the essential instructional guide to life. It is the most comprehensive tutorial on how to live life to the fullest. Wisdom, life skills, and values are what we spend our entire lives seeking. We seek these things through education, job experiences, and relationships—when really the Lord has already provided the perfect how-to literature for us in his written word. "All Scripture is inspired by God and is useful to teach us what is true, and to make us realize what is wrong in our lives. It corrects us when we are wrong and teaches us to do what is right. God uses it to prepare and equip his people to do every good work." (2 Timothy 3:16-17)

Many people say the Bible is antiquated and cannot be applied to modern day culture. But, if we truly are Christians, then we believe the Bible to be true and God's holy, indestructible word. And we also believe that the God who spoke creation into being is the God of yesterday, today, and forever, and his word also stands the test of time. "The grass withers and the flowers fade, but the word of our God stands forever." (Isaiah 40:8). God has not changed, his plan for our lives has not changed, and his word is not only applicable to today's world, but it holds the key ingredients for the recipe that will allow us to live our best life and leave the greatest impact.

The Bible is, first and foremost, meant to point to a God who pursues those he loves, despite their rejection of him. The Bible tells of a God who went to extreme measures, paying the ultimate cost to restore a relationship. The dos and don'ts of the Bible have a dual purpose. First, they function like a mirror to show us that we are unclean and in need of a Savior. And also, once relationship has been restored by a believer's faith in the cross, the Bible serves as wise instruction from a loving father of how we are intended to live.

My goal is not to just highlight biblical principles to bring your life more fulfillment; instead, I want to be a catalyst for you to KNOW JESUS. Biblical principles are essential, but they must be used in correlation with a relationship with Christ!

The topics on the following pages have been designed to cover ten weeks of devotional time, but I encourage you to go at your own pace. Each week tackles a concept that you will encounter along your life's journey. Some concepts may take you more time to work through than others. These are not definitive. They are not resolute. Every journey is unique. Everyone has a different story to tell.

My friend Charis once wrote the following in her blog series *thisonethought*: "This is my real issue with most Christian books: we are mostly opinion. Even when we quote a lot of verses, how we apply them can be opinionated. We can maneuver and manipulate and try to project on our audience the lens through which we see life. The problem is, nobody else has the exact same experience or mentors or childhood or factors that make up that lens...Because, after all, the Truth is not a methodology, a systemized list of rules, or even a philosophy. The Truth is a Person and His name is Jesus."

This blog excerpt perfectly encapsulates my thoughts about this text, and with her permission, I have printed it here. My disclaimer is that I am completely unqualified to have written this devotional. I have no literary degree, no formal training, and I have not participated in any theological study—I just have a heart for the Lord, some stories that illustrate how he has moved in my life, and a calling and desire to share them.

Freije, Charis. "Buy the Truth, and Do Not Sell It." *ThisOneThought*, Blogspot, Aug. 2017, thisonethought.blogspot.com.

MERELY MOVING SHADOWS

Psalms 39:4-7 NLT

A 10-Week Devotional Guide to Living God's Purpose Through His Plan

Katie Stam Irk

Miss America 2009

Merely Moving Shadows

DEVOTIONAL CHALLENGE

Before we get started, please allow me to suggest a challenge to coincide with this devotional.

Consider a fast from social media while completing this study. Why? Fasting is an opportunity to forfeit a "pleasure of the body" to help you not only identify your desire for that item, but also how it competes with your desire to further know the Lord.

During a fast, each time you think of partaking in the item you're going without, pray instead. You will quickly realize how much time, effort, and heart you invest in that item. Fasting helps you recognize where you put your loyalty, and then it takes that loyalty away from that item and places it back with the Lord.

I encourage your fast to be from social media because this will help block distractions as you progress through this study. Blocking distractions will help you become more self-aware, and self-awareness enhances your relationship with Christ. Your relationship with Christ is the foundation for wisdom.

Merely Moving Shadows

CHAPTER ONE
TIMING

Patience. I have really come to dislike the word. In our text message, fast food, live-streaming world, patience feels unnatural. I want it, and I want it now. We all like to say, "It's all in God's timing." But really, we're usually grinding our teeth and muttering under our breath, "But now would be nice!" Living in full surrender to God's timing takes practice, humility, and patience.

I am by nature an entrepreneur. My friends have gotten really good at humoring me each time I start a sentence with, "You know what would be a good idea?" This typically happens about thirty-six times a day, and the sentence usually ends with a new, overly-ambitious idea that I have absolutely NO business doing. We all roll our eyes and laugh, and that's usually the end of it.

However, once upon a time, one of those conversations had quite the surprise ending. I had an idea for a new product line. Even though it seemed preposterous considering I had no experience in the field, I saw the opportunity and dove right in. I developed my idea into a concept, pieced together a presentation, made a few calls, and before long I was meeting with a company who could produce this line. I went in to my meeting expecting to sit down with the marketing team and pitch the idea of being a consultant for them, helping them develop this line and taking it to market. You can imagine my shock when I walked into the conference room and stood in front of every high-ranking executive within the company! After my presentation, the leadership decided my product line was not the right move for them at the time—but they loved me and wanted to bring me on board. I left that meeting with a full-time job, a nice salary, an executive title, benefits, six-weeks paid vacation, and a private office that would be built just for me. It was a dream come true. My job was to develop my own line of products that would be sold through television shopping networks. I was ecstatic, and I couldn't wait to get started.

I spent my first few weeks on the job studying every television shopping network I could find. I wanted to know everything there was to know. My next step was designing my own line to fit the areas of need. I flew across the country to work with our chemist, tour the lab, and research raw ingredients. It took months to piece together and package my first product line, but it was everything I could have hoped for. I was tremendously proud of it, and when the time came to present to the investors, I thought I had hit a homerun.

I was wrong. It was a total strike out. I was confused, and no explanation was given. Reluctantly, I went back to the drawing board. Over the next year, I would develop two more product lines, putting my heart and soul into each one. Each time, I knew I was presenting a top-notch line that was sure to be a success. And each time, I was struck down by the investors. It was incredibly discouraging and immensely frustrating. I felt lost, confused, and angry, and I also felt like my value as a team member was plummeting. In fact, I felt pretty worthless. I had been brought on to complete a very specific task, and although I did my absolute best, no one was buying what I was selling. I connected my perceived failures entirely to my self-worth.

About fourteen months into my employment, I felt a virtual "tap" on my shoulder. I knew the Lord was telling me it was time to go, but I brushed it off. I kept telling myself that he wanted me to have the stability, safety, and security of a regular paycheck, and all the perks that came with my job; not the risk or uncertainty of unemployment! For four months, I neglected the Lord's call away from my job. Every day for four months, I walked in to my office and felt ashamed, worthless, and that I should not be there. I felt the push from every direction, but my stubbornness and worldly desires wouldn't let me leave.

My work environment became incredibly toxic. I constantly wondered if the Lord had led me there to share a little Jesus, but then I noticed that my being there was having the opposite effect: I wasn't falling away from Jesus, but I was falling further away from acting like Jesus. I was wrapped up in a culture in which I didn't believe and to which I did not belong.

Shortly after my final attempt at developing a product line was rejected, the responsibilities of my executive position were relegated to that of an intern. Without a product line in progress, I simply filled in wherever there was a need, picking up odds and ends jobs around the office to feel useful. The Lord was moving me away, but still I resisted.

Finally, eighteen months into my "dream" career, I worked up the nerve to meet with the CEO to offer my resignation. Thankfully, my concerns were well-received and we parted on great terms.

Although it seems as if it all worked out in the end, I still left that job feeling like a total failure and an embarrassment. I felt rejected and ashamed. I felt worthless. I could not understand why God had put me there, only to rip me away a mere year and a half later, leaving me feeling as though I had accomplished nothing.

But, God is good, his promises are true, and his timing is perfect. A short seven months after my departure, the company was turned completely on its head. An extensive investigation was launched to evaluate the day-to-day operations of the business—an investigation that involved the entire executive team, investors, and numerous other employees by association. There had been a massive disagreement for months over how the company was being run, eventually resulting in the termination of each high-ranking executive as well as numerous public lawsuits against each of them. No one, including me, knew whose side to be on, only that they didn't want to be involved.

As the story unfolded, I was on a roller coaster of fear, confusion, and finally, utter relief. The relief came months later as the Lord revealed something to me about that experience. Had any one of my product lines been chosen by the investors, I would have been contractually obligated to this company. I would have launched my new career directly tying my brand and everything I had to this business. There would have been no way out.

The Lord had graced me with his protection.

All I could see during my time in that position was my constant shortcomings. I was impatient with the Lord, wondering why he had even brought me to that company, but now I know. He brought me there because it was a great experience to learn in that work environment, with numerous opportunities to offer provision for my family. I am a better person, businesswoman, and entrepreneur because of that experience, and I have so much to be grateful for. My only regret is not listening to the Lord when he first called me away. Answering his call would have required me to walk away from so much, and I had been placing my trust in the idols I had created for myself: the financial, economic, and social gain found in that position.

These days, my trust belongs and will forever reside in the one true God. I will trust his timing and learn to be patient in his calling. I will trust that when things don't turn out how or when I want, he is in full control and knows exactly what he is doing—and may even have something greater in store.

Our life's journey determines not only our values, our beliefs, our dedication, and our faithfulness, but also our perseverance. Our journey will test us, it will define us, and it requires—or rather, *demands*—patience.

Understanding takes clarity. Clarity takes time. Time takes patience. We wait patiently on the Lord and his truth.

The harsh reality of God's truth, though, is that we may never come to know the why behind many of our life's experiences. Still, we must learn that it is all in God's plan and all in his own timing. We must trust in it. He may lead us down roads that are winding, full of apparent dead-ends, potholes, speed bumps, and traffic jams, but he will always guide us safely to our destination. Along our travels, we can rest peacefully and enjoy the ride no matter how long it takes, knowing he is behind the wheel.

"Wait patiently for the Lord. Be brave and courageous. Yes, wait patiently for the Lord." (Psalms 27:14)

"God's way is perfect. All the Lord's promises prove true. He is a shield for all who look to him for protection." (Psalms 18:30)

"For everything there is a season, a time for every activity under heaven." (Ecclesiastes 3:1)

"Yet God has made everything beautiful for its own time. He has planted eternity in the human heart, but even so, people cannot see the whole scope of God's work from beginning to end." (Ecclesiastes 3:11)

Question & Answer

Trusting in God's Timing

1. What are the desires that drive your life?

2. How do you seek God's kingdom before seeking your own desires?

3. When does your worry come before your faith in God?

4. How can you become more dependent on God?

5. Why does resting or waiting make us feel guilty?

6. What is God trying to teach you while you wait?

7. How can you change your schedule or expectations to prevent you from trying to rush God?

Prayer

Lord God, Heavenly Father, please forgive me for the times when I try to take control. Please forgive me for the moments I take you out of my decision making in an attempt to gain power over my circumstances. Remind me that when I don't understand what is happening, it is all happening by design and that you are the grand designer. Remind me that you knew me before my life began, and you know how my life will end—and all that happens in between. You are my creator and I am your humble servant. Move me where you will. Teach me to rest in your timing. Guide my heart to know and trust you more. Amen.

Personal Prayer Direction

To be a person of faith is to have a relationship with God. You cannot have a relationship with God without communication (prayer). Prayer can seem intimidating, monotonous, or insincere if it's not focused. Writing out prayers or making simple notes can help guide your prayers and direct your conversations with God. Start by answering these two basic questions.

What are you grateful for this week?

Who are you praying for this week?

CHAPTER TWO
BEAUTY

My friend Joy created a beautiful life. She and her husband Jim never had children of their own, but they had countless "adopted" daughters: pageant contestants from every corner of the country who sought interview training for competition from this dynamic duo. I first met Jim and Joy as a seventeen-year-old preparing to compete for Indiana's Junior Miss (now known as Distinguished Young Woman Scholarship Program). I was incredibly nervous as we arrived at their home. They were legendary. Signed photos lined each room and every hallway, depicting the young women Jim and Joy had worked with. Many famous faces with twinkling tiaras and sparkling smiles covered every inch of every wall, with messages of gratitude and love. It was like walking through the most comprehensive, historical pageantry museum ever created. And for every picture, for every success, and for every win, there was a more personal story attached to each young woman.

Jim and Joy never set out to teach anyone how to interview. Instead, they sought to bring out the most beautiful version of each individual by encouraging compassion, building confidence, asserting strength, and empowering boldness. What I learned from them reached further than any competition outcome could ever measure.

As Jim and Joy were lifelong Hoosiers, one of Joy's dreams was to see a Miss Indiana be crowned Miss America. In eighty-eight years, our state had come very close numerous times, but had never taken the crown until 2009. That year, it not only was a fellow Hoosier, but also one of Jim and Joy's "adopted" daughters: it was me. The pageant had brought with it a tremendous amount of excitement and celebration, but shortly after everyone returned home, we got the devastating news: Joy would be battling breast cancer, a horrible battle that she had valiantly and victoriously fought before. After having been in remission for several years and overcoming several other serious medical obstacles in that time, Joy was about to face the giant again; but this time, the giant had come prepared to win.

Due to the extensive travel and work schedule I was keeping after being crowned, it was difficult to keep up with the latest updates on Joy's health. I didn't know how extreme her condition had become throughout the course of that year, mostly because she never allowed anyone to see just how bad it was. No matter how hard things had become and no matter how bad it hurt, Joy's attitude never wavered; she never gave in. Instead of allowing treatment to take her hair, Joy shaved it off to show cancer that *she* was the one in control. Instead of giving in to the loss of strength, Joy never missed a beat and kept up with her active life, participating in as much as she could. She lived each day with a spirit of light, a spirit of hope, and a spirit of, well...Joy. She found the beauty in her battle.

Before I traveled to Las Vegas to crown the next Miss America in 2010, I was given the opportunity to come back to Indiana to finalize details of my new, "normal" life. Apartment searching, car buying, and job hunting were all on the docket for the short time that I would be home. I was fully immersed in my preparations for life after the crown when I got word that Joy had passed—the day before I left to go back to the pageant. I truly believe that Joy waited until the last possible second. She wanted to see every moment of her Miss Indiana as Miss America. When the time came for me to leave for Las Vegas to pass on the title, Joy knew she could pass in peace. For Joy, the Miss America title could stay right at home in Indiana!

Cancer is ugly. Fighting cancer is uglier. Losing the fight or losing someone to cancer is the ugliest. How do you find beauty in the midst of such a defeating battle? Joy did. I don't remember Joy being sick, but I do remember the spunky, sassy, victorious spirit that remained in her until the very end. It lives on today in the lives of those she touched.

I once met a man that reminded me a lot of Joy; who upon being asked if he was having a bad day, replied, "I never have bad days, just bad moments!" Genius. Never give a bad moment the power to ruin your entire day. This man understood the influence of your thoughts and attitude. He understood the concept of living with a spirit of Joy. He understood how to find the beauty in every situation, no matter how desperate. It's ok to have bad moments. It's even ok to have bad days. However, you must realize that the situation you have fought or are currently fighting is only temporary.

Don't make a permanent decision based on temporary pain.

Don't let pain be your perspective-let it be beauty and joy instead.

Beauty and joy come from God's perfect love. The Bible says that God's perfect love casts out all fears. The Bible tells us that our light and momentary sufferings pale in comparison to the eternal joy we will experience with Jesus, and that God is working out all things for the ultimate good of those who love him, even when we can't see how, because God's ways are higher than our ways. He does sometimes intervene and work miracles on our behalf, but more often than not, he intervenes by offering himself and his love in ever-increasing measure. This is the reason we can be joyful.

Sometimes, our journey can get ugly. Really ugly. But through the tears and the trials, we must find the beauty. No matter how hard it is, find the beauty. When you can't find it, create something beautiful.

"Don't be concerned about the outward beauty of fancy hairstyles, expensive jewelry, or beautiful clothes. You should clothe yourselves instead with the beauty that comes from within, the unfading beauty of a gentle and quiet spirit, which is so precious to God." (1 Peter 3:3-4)

"Charm is deceptive, and beauty does not last; but a woman who fears the Lord will be greatly praised." (Proverbs 31:30)

"Since God chose you to be the holy people he loves, you must clothe yourselves with tenderhearted mercy, kindness, humility, gentleness, and patience." (Colossians 3:12)

"Dear brothers and sisters, when troubles of any kind come your way, consider it an opportunity for great joy. For you know that when your faith is tested, your endurance has a chance to grow. So, let it grow, for when your endurance is fully developed, you will be perfect and complete, needing nothing . . . God blesses those who patiently endure testing and temptation. Afterward they will receive the crown of life that God has promised to those who love him." (James 1:2-4, 12)

Question & Answer

Finding the Beauty

1. What does the word *beauty* mean to you?

2. What do you think makes a person beautiful?

3. What do you think people mean when they say that beauty is in the eye of the beholder?

4. What can you let go of right now that will allow you to be more joyful?

5. What can you do or say right now that will generate joy?

6. How can you put joy, beauty, and appreciation into practice in your everyday life?

7. Is there a difference between joy and happiness?

Prayer

Heavenly Father, help me find beauty. Help me see past my pain, my troubles, and my losses to put on an attitude of joy, grace, and positivity. Show me the beauty you have created around me and forgive me for not being able or willing to see it on my own. Lord, only you have the power to heal my wounds. Heal my heart and teach me how to help others heal. Although I may bear scars as reminders of my pain, I pray that the display of my scars be a testament to your faithfulness in my life. Use my journey so that others may find beauty through their trials as well. Amen.

Personal Prayer Direction

What are you grateful for this week?

Who are you praying for this week?

Merely Moving Shadows

CHAPTER THREE
FORGIVENESS

Forgiveness is hard. Period. Sometimes, it's seemingly impossible. When someone hurts us, it's easy to think that forgiveness consists of basically telling them, "It's ok. You're off the hook." I don't know about you, but even writing those words makes me feel the anger start to rise within me, along with my blood pressure. However, we should remember that God's forgiveness is not telling people what they did is ok. He would never condone sin. God's forgiveness is saying to those who hurt you: "I will love you through it, and despite it."

I have many illustrations of forgiveness from my life's journey. I have walked many rough roads. I have been bullied, lied to, cheated, manipulated, stolen from, sexually harassed, abused, put down, left out, taken advantage of, and rejected.

I have also been a perpetrator of many of these aforementioned sins. I have made many poor decisions and have used poor judgment in many situations. I have been the source of hurt and pain, and for that, I sincerely repent.

I could use this chapter to tell stories of my trials or my sorrows, but that is not a reflection of forgiveness. There are times in our lives when we are faced with conflict, and we must decide whether we are going to be a part of the problem or a part of the solution. Retelling our stories of hurt and pain does not change the hurt or the pain, but speaking of the transformative power of forgiveness does.

I am choosing to not tell the story that is the greatest example of forgiveness from my life. This is an unusual decision to say the least and one that does not come lightly. My reasons are for protection of the individuals involved as well as to ensure the emphasis of this chapter to be on why and how to forgive. Simply put: This book is not about my stories. It is about our redeeming Father. The stories I share are simply reflections of God's mighty works that I have witnessed firsthand. With that being said, I would like to focus on the act of forgiveness.

Forgiveness starts with a posture of humility. After all, we are undeserving of the grace shown to us by a holy and perfect God. If God, who is without blemish, can forgive us, then we should be able to forgive others for their sins against us. Our posture must reflect the knowledge that we are first, sinners; and second, sinned-against. We are able to forgive others because God, in all his righteousness, first forgave us.

This is not intended to, in any way, create a sense of guilt or to lessen the hurt you may have endured. Some people have experienced true evil in their lives, living through horrors that can only be described as hell on earth. I affirm your hurt and pain. I grieve with you, and I pray for repentance of the perpetrator and for reconciliation and peace. For many, it seems that forgiveness is not an option; that forgiveness is too kind to offer an unkind, undeserving individual, even if they are offering repentance. However, the choice to forgive does not and should not rely on another's actions, or lack thereof. It has been said that beauty lies in the eye of the beholder; so, too, does forgiveness. It is something that must happen within us.

Forgiveness is not a feeling—it is a decision you make. It is a decision to not allow the hurt to control your life, your outlook, or your relationships. It is a decision to move on, and in some cases, to move *away* from the abuse, neglect, or pain. The Lord calls us to forgive, but he does NOT call us to remain in an abusive situation. Remove yourself from that place, person, or circumstance and find solace in the comfort of family, friends, and prayer. Pray for the Lord's continued protection. Pray for the Holy Spirit to transform your heart to allow room for forgiveness. Pray over those who have hurt you. Pray for their own knowledge of their actions and words. Pray for their repentance and pray that they seek the Lord.

It's time to let go of the hurt, pain, anger, frustration, and sadness. What do these feelings offer you? If someone has hurt you in the past, harboring negative feelings toward them is like drinking poison but expecting them to get sick. Forgiveness is one of the greatest gifts we could ever offer *or* receive from another person, and it is also the greatest gift we can give ourselves.

Are you tired of your bad memories bringing death to your life? Forgiveness is hard. It seems impossible. But it is so powerful. It is the most powerful action you could ever take towards another human being or for yourself. AND, it's possible with God.

No story of mine could replicate the most powerful demonstration of forgiveness better than Jesus's sacrifice and death on the cross. Although Jesus lived a perfect life, he suffered in unimaginable ways in order to pay for our sins. Though Jesus was innocent, he did not call down judgment from the cross. Instead, he offered forgiveness. In Luke 23:34, Jesus said, "Father, forgive them, for they know not what they do." Even in the midst of his suffering, moments before his death, Jesus offered forgiveness to those who had beaten and bruised him, mocked him, dug a crown of thorns into his head, tortured him, and nailed him to a cross.

When you feel as though you have no option but to succumb to the pain of your past, remember that God has blessed you with so many beautiful gifts. Forgiveness is by far the most expensive gift he has given us. It cost the crucifixion of his only son. It is the gift that can bring us comfort and peace. It is the greatest reflection of God's love, and it offers the promise of eternal life in heaven with him.

When we believe we don't have the strength or capacity to forgive, we must trust that the Lord will cover our shortcomings and fill our gaps. He will make up for our discrepancies. With his loving kindness and grace, we can be healed—and we can heal the world. Forgiveness is the cure.

"Make allowance for each other's faults, and forgive anyone who offends you. Remember, the Lord forgave you, so you must forgive others." (Colossians 3:13)

"Get rid of all bitterness, rage, anger, harsh words, and slander, as well as all types of evil behavior. Instead, be kind to each other, tenderhearted, forgiving one another, just as God through Christ has forgiven you." (Ephesians 4:31-32)

"So watch yourselves! 'If another believer sins, rebuke that person; then if there is repentance, forgive. Even if that person wrongs you seven times a day and each time turns again and asks forgiveness, you must forgive.'" (Luke 17:3-4)

"No, dear brothers and sisters, I have not achieved it, but I focus on this one thing: Forgetting the past and looking forward to what lies ahead, I press on to reach the end of the race and receive the heavenly prize for which God, through Christ Jesus, is calling us." (Philippians 3:13-14)

"If you forgive those who sin against you, your heavenly Father will forgive you. But if you refuse to forgive others, your Father will not forgive your sins." (Matthew 6:14-15)

Question & Answer

Choosing Forgiveness

1. What does forgiveness mean to you?

2. Is forgiveness conditional? Are there unforgiveable sins, or reasons why someone shouldn't receive forgiveness?

3. When you forgive, are you condoning sin?

4. Is forgiveness required even when there isn't repentance?

5. How do you forgive when you simply don't want to?

Prayer

Dear Lord, teach me to forgive. Soften my heart. When I can't get past the hurt or when I can't see past the pain, open my eyes to see you and your love. Help me extend grace when I don't believe someone deserves it. Help me extend grace to myself when I don't believe I deserve it. I praise you for your unrelenting forgiveness and for your blood, which covers all my sin. You love me despite my mistakes. Help me love others despite their mistakes. Lord, search the hearts of those who have hurt me in the past. Help them to acknowledge their sins, acknowledge the pain they inflicted, and sincerely repent. Help me to always choose forgiveness, Lord. When it seems impossible, help me choose forgiveness. Amen.

Personal Prayer Direction

What are you grateful for this week?

Who are you praying for this week?

Merely Moving Shadows

CHAPTER FOUR
STRENGTH

As Miss America 2009, I had the incredible honor of serving as the national goodwill ambassador of Children's Miracle Network Hospitals. CMNH is a fundraising organization that financially assists a large network of children's hospitals, ensuring that no child is turned away regardless of their ability to pay. My time spent as the national goodwill ambassador remains some of the most life-changing and rewarding work of my life. Many of the children and families I met through that experience remain close to my heart, and they serve as some of my greatest sources of inspiration and influence.

People ask me regularly how I was able to complete that work without showing my emotions. Being surrounded by children who are battling life-threatening illnesses and who may also be losing their hair, have atrophied muscles, could be hooked up to a number of life-saving machines, and are showcasing scars with unimaginable origins would be justification for any level of emotional breakdown. My answer has always been the same: the kids don't let you be sad. Despite overcoming tremendous physical obstacles, the children with whom I came into contact always presented a smile, a positive attitude, and an excitement about each new day.

Each time I was sent to a new hospital to tour, meet children, sign autographs, play a game, or read a story with the kids, I was meant to bring a little bit of joy to each of them. However, *I* always felt like the one walking away with a breath of new life. It never seemed fair; having gained so much more than I could have possibly given. What I learned from those children and families continues to direct my path, and I will carry those lessons with me forever.

Families who have sick children are the epitome of strength. You cannot convince me otherwise.

Nearly halfway through my year of service I was brought in for a hospital visit. The usual team of representatives met together to discuss the day's itinerary: a quick tour, spending some time in the child-life center, followed by some media and a short presentation. Little did I know what was truly in store for me that day. My initial tour went exactly as planned. Next, I was escorted to the NICU to visit some of the families being treated there. The NICU is especially difficult. As I entered the NICU, I was immediately greeted by a family of four: a father, mother, their teenage daughter, and daughter of about seven approached me to say hello. The family was clearly in distress, and the mother's face portrayed a story of great grief and sadness. I was not briefed on the current situation prior; however, it became instantly clear that something very serious was happening. The next few moments unfolded very quickly and effortlessly. After exchanging a few pleasantries, we hugged, and then we joined hands, one next to the other as their ten-day-old son and brother was taken off of life support just a few feet away. The baby had been born with numerous, serious deficiencies, and there was a zero percent chance of survival. The family knew his fate early on in the pregnancy, but they chose to endure. Understanding that they would be facing this inevitable fear didn't make it any easier to withstand their loss. We stood together, clutching each other's hand as we looked on at a life that never had a chance to live; I, attempting to transmit every ounce of my strength to the mother. We watched. We waited. We wept as the good Lord welcomed him home.

It is sobering to reflect on that family and our intense moments together. When I think about them, I'm reminded of their calm demeanors, their defeated, yet grateful expressions that extended from their heart, and their ever-present strength in that moment. The powerful clasp of their hands, their confident stature, their collected emotions: it was the presence of the Lord in their lives. The Lord was carrying them in that moment. Each moment the mother wanted to let her knees give out, allowing her to collapse into a pool of grief over her dying newborn son, she stood erect, instead, with an air of peace about her. The Lord was holding her up, supporting her. It was the full surrender to the Lord and his promises that kept that mother going, pushing through for her daughters, her husband, and her son. The time spent in the NICU that day has been impressed so boldly upon my heart.

Strength is needed in times of stress, grief, and fear. When we feel as though we are not strong enough to endure on our own, we must reach out and grab the Father's hand to assist us. He is by our side and will stand with us through the

41

fight. If we believe we are too weak to even reach out, he will simply pick us up and carry us just as he did for that mother in the NICU. The trick is that we must allow him to do so.

I have used the common phrase many times before that the Lord doesn't give us anything we can't handle. While I believe this phrase to be true, I don't believe that I have always used the phrase in its entirety. In all actuality, the Lord doesn't give us anything we can't handle *without him*. We must learn to lean on him. We must trust that he is the source of our strength and our completeness. He will guide us on our path, provide the tools necessary to endure the hardships, and bring us safely home.

"But the Lord is faithful; he will strengthen you and guard you from the evil one." *(*2 Thessalonians 3:3)

"Give your burdens to the Lord, and he will take care of you. He will not permit the godly to slip and fall." (Psalms 55:22)

"My health may fail, and my spirit may grow weak, but God remains the strength of my heart; he is mine forever." (Psalms 73:26)

"I love you, Lord; you are my strength. The Lord is my rock, my fortress, and my savior; my God is my rock, in whom I find protection. He is my shield, the power that saves me, and my place of safety." (Psalms 18:1-2)

Question & Answer

<u>Stand Firm with Strength</u>

1. When was a time you fully surrendered to the Lord for strength in a tough situation?

2. Name a situation you are currently in that is an obstacle for you and requires strength.

3. List the facts of that situation.

4. List the feelings of that situation.

5. Is there a solution to overcoming the obstacle?

6. If yes to #5, is the solution yours to solve?

7. What can you do to stand firm in the Lord's strength and move forward through this trial?

Prayer

Heavenly Father, give me strength to endure life's trials. There have been so many times I have felt like giving up and giving in to my desperation. I can't do it on my own. There have been so many times I have felt inadequately prepared to overcome my obstacles. Remind me that you are the source of my strength. You are my anchor. Hold me tight to your truth. I know that you are always with me. Be my light, be my sight, and be my strength, Lord. Amen.

Personal Prayer Direction

What are you grateful for this week?

Who are you praying for this week?

CHAPTER FIVE
DISCONTENTMENT

I wish I had a single, extraordinarily profound story that illustrates a time when God taught me a lesson about being discontent. The truth is, I have about 1,784,472. Discontentment deals with nearly every single one of the Ten Commandments: idolatry, coveting, stealing, killing, adultery, gossip, and dishonor. Our sins can all be traced back to discontentment. Discontentment affects us physically, emotionally, and mentally, all which affect our judgment. Poor judgment leads to sin.

It is human nature to always want more. Look at the history of our portion sizes, the sizes of our homes, our salaries, or our waist lines. They all seem to get bigger because we are always left wanting—or so we have trained ourselves to feel. We must deal with our discontentment. It is only then that we can truly rest in the Lord and find the happiness that he delights in for us. (More on that at the end of the chapter)

In March of 2016, I started my sixth business. My career had become a potpourri of real estate, technology and consulting endeavors, with four additional projects and business ideas I was actively pursuing—all while being a wife and mother. I thought I was such a go-getter; ambitious and out to conquer the world! The reality was that my drive, my prosperity, or my sharp business acumen weren't behind these pursuits; instead, it was my discontentment.

One particular day, I was feeling extremely bogged down and defeated by my schedule when I had an epiphany. I asked myself if the reason I had six businesses was because I was a superwoman with super human dreams, or because I was a little lost and didn't really know what to do with my life. The answer was really hard to swallow. I was a little lost, and I was discontent with where my life was. I had come to a fork in the road, where being Miss America seemed like ancient history and being Mom didn't seem like enough. Yes, I said it: I didn't feel like I was doing enough as a mom. I wanted so badly for it to be enough for me, but I was so discontent that I found myself in an identity crisis. I spent countless nights doodling in a journal and sending up prayers, asking God to make it apparent to me what I was supposed to do with my life and who I was supposed to be. For weeks, I was drowning in a desire for something more, but I had no idea what that something was.

My thirtieth birthday was right around the corner. Impeccable timing for an identity crisis, right? It was a significant birthday. The teenage years are when you start to assert your independence, but they bring with them some immaturity and irresponsibility. In your twenties, you typically become fully independent. You grow in maturity and responsibility, but slip-ups are expected. To me, thirty was when one became a true adult and would have all the answers. So, why did I feel so lost and confused?

I really am blessed with the most amazing husband. Brian saw my despair and came up with the perfect idea for my birthday. He gifted me a scrapbook filled with letters from thirty of my closest friends, family, mentors, and role models. These letters shared anecdotal stories and emotional moments, with pictures attached. Some were even covered with glitter, original artwork, and jewels. It was a collection of each of these individuals' personalities on paper, and it meant the world to me. I cried the entire time as I read every word, twice over dinner. While reading through the letters, I started to notice a common phrase; it was like the Lord had highlighted it for me. Numerous people had written in their letters that I had made them feel special. Those words humbled me, and also charged me with action. I had been waiting for the Lord to reveal to me what I was supposed to do with my life, and it was staring me in the face on the pages in front of me. I was to make people feel special. It didn't matter how, but the Lord made me to make others feel special; to be a constant reminder that they are precious creations and blessings, and that there is a God who loves them so much.

After my birthday, I was resolved. I quickly dissolved one of my businesses as I knew it wasn't the right move; an effort with all the wrong intention. Several weeks later, I dissolved a second business. I was simplifying my life—or at least, the job portions of it—and focusing my energy into how I could use what God had already put in my life to be an encouragement to others. I stopped chasing the goal of heaping up financial wealth, and instead began working to heap up heavenly wealth, attempting to win people for Jesus.

I wanted to let his light shine through every conversation I had and every action I took, all with the intent of making others feel special. This personal experience caused me to pause and reflect on the other areas of discontentment in my life: my appearance, my home, my wardrobe, my vehicle, my finances, and so much more.

The main reason we feel discontentment is because we are constantly searching for something that will make us happy, instead of finding happiness in what we already have. I stated at the beginning of this chapter that the Lord delights in our happiness, and he does; but the Lord does not call us to be happy. Nowhere in the Bible will you read, "And the Lord called out to them and said, 'Just do what makes you happy!'" The Lord does not call us to do what makes us happy; he calls us to do what is right. Doing what is right is not always easy, and it takes courage. When we are obedient to his word, we can rest with contentment. Contentment leads to happiness.

Are you dealing with discontentment? Not just with your physical appearance, possessions or job, but possibly with your marriage, your friendships, or maybe your attitude? Our society has warped our minds into believing we can never settle or find peace, at least without a purchase. We are promised products that can create fullness, and if we don't feel fulfilled by that product, we should just keep buying. We must understand and acknowledge that we live in a distorted perception of need versus want. What do we really need? What will provide us true contentment? The answer is Jesus's love. And here's the best part: his love is **free**, unconditional, always readily available, and never runs out. It's an endless supply for an ever-increasing demand. Don't you wish all we ever craved was more of Jesus? Ask yourself: is there really anything else that truly matters?

"After all, we brought nothing with us when we came into the world, and we can't take anything with us when we leave it. So if we have enough food and clothing, let us be content. But people who long to be rich fall into temptation and are trapped by many foolish and harmful desires that plunge them into ruin and destruction. For the love of money is the root of all kinds of evil. And some people, craving money, have wandered from the true faith and pierced themselves with many sorrows." (1 Timothy 6:7-10)

"By his divine power, God has given us everything we need for living a godly life. We have received all of this by coming to know him, the one who called us to himself by means of his marvelous glory and excellence. And because of his glory and excellence, he has given us great and precious promises. These are the promises that enable you to share his divine nature and escape the world's corruption caused by human desires." (2 Peter 1:3-4)

"So what do people get in this life for all their hard work and anxiety? Their days of labor are filled with pain and grief; even at night their minds cannot rest. It is all meaningless. So I decided there is nothing better than to enjoy food and drink and to find satisfaction in work. Then I realized that these pleasures are from the hand of God. For who can eat or enjoy anything apart from him?" (Ecclesiastes 2:22-25)

"Don't love money; be satisfied with what you have. For God has said, 'I will never fail you. I will never abandon you.'" (Hebrews 13:5)

Question & Answer

Dealing with Discontentment

1. What makes you feel discontent?

2. What do you believe will solve your discontentment?

3. Could creating different conditions, items, or environments make you more content?

    3a. If yes: Do you believe that solution is something God would want?

    3b. If no: What can make life better?

4. What would it take for you to be satisfied? Could God provide that? Should he?

Prayer

Father God, teach me to be content in you. It's so easy to get caught up in always wanting and feeling like I need more. Help me correctly identify the source of my discontentment and silence that source. Help me turn a blind eye to the promises of this world, and help me to fully trust in the promise of your provision. Teach me to rest contently in your word and in your love. You are enough. Take this world Lord, and give me more of you. Amen.

Personal Prayer Direction

What are you grateful for this week?

Who are you praying for this week?

Merely Moving Shadows

CHAPTER SIX

FEAR

I have struggled with this week's topic for some time, fighting an inner battle over whether to tackle stress or fear. After some deliberation, I came to realize that fear really is the root of all stress. We feel stressed over our fear of not having enough time to complete tasks. We feel stressed over our children, fearing we have not equipped them with the proper nutrients, skills, or resources to succeed and thrive. We feel stressed when we fear our finances will not cover our debts. If we tackle fear, we tackle stress; therefore, let's focus on facing fear, understanding where it comes from and how to live fearlessly.

It took me two years to be able to tell the following story. I consider myself to be a strong, courageous woman, but this story is about my greatest weakness: my fear over the well-being of my children. That makes me vulnerable, which in turn makes me afraid.

In May 2015, my husband and I welcomed our second child, Rose. She was two days overdue, a whopping 8 pounds, 5 ounces with a head full of jet-black hair. Our spunky, sassy, sweet little girl would be the perfect addition to our family. Everything was normal during delivery. We spent our standard two days in the hospital where she passed every test available. Being a mother to a newborn again seemed to fall right back into place for me.

We were released to go home on a Wednesday night. We arrived home to smiling faces and a very proud big sister around 8:30 p.m. We enjoyed a swing on the front porch, listening to the sounds of spring and cleansing our palettes of hospital sterility. As the night progressed, Rose had a difficult time settling in. She seemed extremely uncomfortable, and as we moved into the early morning hours, she became quite agitated, screaming endlessly and scalding hot to the touch. I couldn't figure out what was wrong with my baby. We initially feared Rose may be frustrated with extracting thick colostrum while nursing, so Brian ran out to purchase some formula. However, our attempt at the bottle only made her angrier.

Finally, we decided to take her temperature. It was 100.8°F, and my heart sank. I remembered reading that any temperature in a newborn is cause to call the pediatrician immediately, so Brian and I called two different ones we had previously seen. Both ordered us to the emergency room. We quickly packed a bag and arrived at the ER around 3:00 a.m. The moment we entered the hospital room, something felt off. The doctors and nurses immediately informed us about the statewide protocol that requires a series of five tests for any infant under the age of three months who runs a fever as it is typically a clear sign of infection.

They were going to start with a spinal tap. **Start with a spinal tap**. My two-day old baby spiked a fever, something she biologically shouldn't even be capable of doing at her age, was most likely fighting off a major infection, and was currently undergoing a procedure during which a doctor would draw brain fluid through a needle inserted into her spine. I cannot accurately depict my state at that current time; I was so afraid. My body was numb. I excused myself from the ER while the procedure was taking place, as I knew I wouldn't be able to withstand the sight. I requested that my husband remain to oversee it and be there for our Rosie. And although I couldn't bring myself to be in the room, I also couldn't be too far away. Instead, I sat outside the door, panic-stricken, bent over, arms crossed, bobbing up and down with tears streaming down my face, yelling for God to give me whatever had invaded my child's body. I heard every scream and every cry from that hospital room, and I matched it with one of my own during every painful, passing second. Twice, nurses approached me, offering me condolences and hugs to calm the fear.

The moment the door opened, I raced back to my baby girl's side. I'll never be able to block out the image of Rosie lying there on her side, limp from exhaustion. The tools from the doctor's kit lay on a blood-spotted towel next to her. The hospital staff excused themselves to allow us a moment of peace. Brian hesitantly leaned over to share with me that the procedure was unsuccessful—and that they would have to make another attempt shortly. I couldn't contain my anger. I threw myself on my baby girl, stroking her head, insisting that God not allow that to happen. As angry and as scared as I was in those moments, the terror was really just beginning. I was petrified listening to the nurses describe the next steps when they came back into the room, which was extracting urine and blood samples and starting an IV of medicine to treat whatever infection she was fighting. There were so many special tools, needles, and bandages, I couldn't see straight.

There were screams, tears, weakness, discomfort, painful pricks, and blown blood vessels and it was all adding up to one failure after the next. Before we knew it, we had finished four of the five procedures, and not a single one was performed successfully. I became a zombie. Watching my baby girl be treated like a guinea pig was unbearable. The last procedure was a chest x-ray. How could they mess that up? Thankfully, they didn't.

We were given a few more minutes of rest before the doctors were to come back to re-try their failed attempts in an effort to collect the rest of the data necessary for testing. However, this time a new set of nurses walked into our hospital room. They were from the Neonatal Intensive Care Unit (NICU) at the hospital, and they had brought with them some brand new equipment created specifically to handle newborn cases like these. One after another, each procedure was a success, with the exception of the spinal tap. Fortunately, the NICU nurses told us that procedure would wait for another day. Praise God!

We were admitted to the NICU for the next five days while test results were being processed. Fear controlled my every thought, my every action, and my every heartbeat for those five days. I lived in fear of the worst.

Over the next five days, each test result came back negative. Rosie was responding well to the antibiotics she was receiving and the doctors were astounded at her body's resilience. With each passing day and new test result, the doctors became more optimistic about her condition, eventually deciding that an additional spinal tap would be unnecessary. Hallelujah! Good news met with exceptional care from our new doctors and nurses during our stay in the NICU.

Doctors were never able to explain what was happening in Rose's body, nor what had seemed to cure her. I know what happened. Miracles don't need explanation. I asked God to heal her, and it's simple: he did. I have a healthy, funny, boisterous, smart, kind, little girl who brings me so much light and laughter, thanks to the healing power of Jesus.

You've probably heard that the phrase *do not fear* is mentioned more than one hundred times in the Bible. It is a clear message that the Lord has not given us a spirit of fear, but instead, we are called to live our lives in confidence, comforted in the knowledge that his mighty power is available to each and every one of us and is accessible at any moment.

I praise God that he healed my baby girl. I could be telling a much different story; a story filled with so much more heartache. A story I have walked through with close friends, after they have lost children who had suffered through sickness and unknown ailments, or had children who battled aggressive cancers. I feel tremendously blessed to be able to tell my story, and I am at a loss for words on how to describe my sympathy to those whose stories had different endings. The Lord says in the Bible, "Ask and ye shall receive." I don't understand why it seems like some prayers go unanswered, or seem to come with an answer of no. But I do know that through the darkness, the Lord heals, he restores, and he renews. Don't give up hope.

Every day, we are attacked by the enemy, allowing fear to enter our world in some way. Fear steals our joy and robs us of our precious time, forcing us to constantly be drowning in the thoughts of what if and what's next. We must be able to identify that fear is what the devil wants from us, because fear prevents us from living our full potential for the Lord. Fear is cumbersome and even paralyzing. It surrounds us, covers us, and can suffocate us. When we start to sink into our fear, we are buying into the lies of the devil. We must be able to call him out by name and demand that he flee from us—and that he take his fear with him.

Fear creates isolation. Isolation surrounds us in darkness. As children we learn to sing, "This little light of mine, I'm gonna let it shine!" The older we get, the more disconnected we become to the youthfulness of that song; yet we still remember the lyrics, and maybe even the hand motions. Don't you think there's a reason this song is taught to us when we are young? It's simple; yet powerful, memorable, and poignant. Jesus is the light. Jesus lives in us; therefore, his light is in us. Let his light shine brightly in the darkness, and don't let Satan blow it out! Let it shine.

Don't let your fear be bigger than your faith.

Loes, Harry Dixon. "This little light of mine." *Public Domain* (1920).

"The Lord is my light and my salvation-so why should I be afraid? The Lord is my fortress, protecting me from danger, so why should I tremble? When evil people come to devour me, when my enemies and foes attack me, they will stumble and fall. Though a mighty army surrounds me, my heart will not be afraid. Even if I am attacked, I will remain confident." (Psalms 27:1-3)

"See, God has come to save me. I will trust in him and not be afraid. The Lord God is my strength and my song; he has given me victory." (Isaiah 12:2)

"The Lord says, 'I will rescue those who love me. I will protect those who trust in my name. When they call on me, I will answer; I will be with them in trouble. I will rescue and honor them.'" (Psalms 91:14-16)

"'I have told you all this so that you may have peace in me. Here on earth you will have many trials and sorrows. But take heart, because I have overcome the world.'" (John 16:33)

Question & Answer

Identifying Fear

1. What are your greatest fears, excluding things like snakes, spiders, heights, and ghosts?

2. What fears are you facing right now?

3. When we are fearful, it's usually because we fear the actual process of going through something, or because we fear the final outcome. Which are you most fearful of in the circumstance you listed above: the process or the outcome? (example: Starting a new business. Are you more afraid of the process i.e. the learning curves or heavier work load, or are you more afraid of the business failing altogether?)
You can fear both the process and the outcome. This question is an effort to help us identify the root of our fear.

4. Are you concerned with your ability to handle either the process or the outcome?

5. Is there anything mentally, physically, or emotionally that prevents you from being equipped to handle either the process or outcome? If so, is it possible that you are hearing the devil tell you that you are inadequate?

6. Are you trying to protect yourself from either the process or outcome?

Prayer

Heavenly Father, teach me to live fearlessly. Regardless of my current circumstance, Lord, help me keep my eyes on you. Help me to trust your will no matter what happens. You know what I am walking through, Lord, and you know the depths of my heart; the feelings I cannot communicate. Only you fully understand, and only you can truly heal this brokenness. When I feel paralyzed by my fear, grant me peace to know that you are in control. And, Lord I pray that you instill in me the knowledge that I am equipped to handle whatever life throws my way, because you are my constant and eternal guide, my protection, my restoration, and my light. Amen.

Personal Prayer Direction

What are you grateful for this week?

Who are you praying for this week?

CHAPTER SEVEN
CONVICTION

In 2011, I was invited to be the keynote speaker at a national women's annual conference. I was ecstatic to work with the group and headline their captive audience of over five-thousand. This convention was tremendously important to me, and I prepared for weeks in advance. I researched. I crafted my message. I rehearsed. I timed myself and noted those times down to the second in my script. I was prepared, or so I thought.

I was brought in the night before the main event in order to explore the convention. Upon arrival, I attended a church service held in the same arena where I was to speak in the very next evening. I was looking forward to learning the acoustics, meeting the group to whom I was presenting, and getting a feel for the general theme of the weekend's festivities. The evening was magical. I can still hear the thousands of female voices singing *Amazing Grace* in unison, acapella. The worship echoed through the stadium, and it still echoes in my memory. I couldn't help but be moved to tears, pouring out my voice for the Lord in that inspiring, powerful, and awe-filled moment. The Holy Spirit was ever-present and permeated every inch of that cavernous building.

The title message for the evening was "Living on the Edge." The pastor spoke intensely about our calling to live on the edge for Jesus; capitalizing on every moment. I sat frozen in my seat, hanging on to every word. Throughout his entire message; however, I started to feel ashamed. Conviction. It was stinging me with every syllable of his sermon. Conviction. Have I really done enough for my Lord? Am I doing enough for my Lord? Am I truly living on the edge for my Lord? I was preparing to speak in front of 5,000 women about my journey of faith, serving as an example of a "Christian life well-lived," and I felt like a phony.

Immediately upon return to my hotel room that night, I shredded my previously prepared, researched, rehearsed, timed script. Then I picked up a pen and paper and started writing, and I didn't stop writing until the moment I took the stage the next evening for my presentation! Here's what I shared

"That little word conviction has been sticking around me for quite some time now...If tomorrow were the end of the world as we know it, have I done everything I wanted to do on Earth before entering

Heaven? I started thinking, what is it I haven't done yet that I must before Judgment Day? I immediately thought of two things and even after some time of allowing that thought to simmer, I stick with my initial two. I have always wanted to be a mother. I was born to be a mother and I cannot wait to start my family. The second thing is that I have never read my Bible (in its entirety). How dare I? To stand in front of my maker someday and not have read his scripture fully would be shameful. I have taken on idols I have allowed to steal my attention and time ... I once heard that if you read three chapters of your Bible every day, you will read the entire thing in a year. I don't want another year to go by before finishing this goal.

Another moment of conviction came a few weeks back in my Bible study group. My pastor wanted us to do an activity in preparation for our discussion. We were to choose an event in the future where people would get up to speak about you. We were to answer the following questions: Where am I? What character traits do others use to describe me? What does my spouse say? What do my children say? What do my friends say? I started filling this out. I chose my husband's and my 50th anniversary. I put a lot of time and effort into each question. And, when I got to the last question, I stopped dead in my tracks. What would my friends say at my wedding anniversary? The reason I paused was because I couldn't think of very many friends who would be there. I am so focused on investing in my family and in my business relationships, yet I invest no time or energy into people and friendships outside of those areas. It's amazing how a person who spends very little time alone can be so lonely. Yes, I am very busy, but we make time for the things we really want to do. I have too many text messages, voicemails and emails that go unanswered because I am 'too busy.' I might as well spit in the face of old friends trying to rekindle a friendship. Again, how dare I? God blesses our lives with relationships and friendships that bring so much joy to us, and not answering is just as bad as bluntly turning them away!

The latest conviction most recently was brought on through last night's worship service, but has been eating away at me for weeks. I started reading the book The One Thing You Can't Do in Heaven by Mark Cahill within the last few weeks. The author describes the one thing you cannot do in Heaven as witnessing to a nonbeliever because there are no nonbelievers in Heaven. His purpose is to inspire, encourage and motivate you to be a better witness for the Lord. He offers incredible stories from personal experiences that will fill your heart, and also offers resources and ideas on how to start the conversation, and more importantly WHY you should start the conversation. After reading portions of this book, the thought came to my head that I grew up in a family who was the

Cahill, Mark. *One Thing You Can't Do in Heaven*. Biblical Discipleship Publishers, 2011.

epitome of JOY (Jesus, Others, and then You), taught me about my Savior and continues to feed me spiritually. What did I ever do to earn that? Nothing. I had no choice in the matter just as those who were born into an atheist or agnostic family, or those who have never heard the good news before in their life.

Where would I be if someone had not shown me God's love? I am not doing God's work if the only places I go to witness are churches, parochial schools and church-affiliated events like these. I was convicted to live on the edge to go outside of my comfort zone to witness. I have had two opportunities lately God provided for me to witness to a stranger. Both on an airplane, and I didn't take the opportunity! I froze when the conversation allowed an opening.

Last night we heard about people in Bible times that were living on the edge for their Lord, and they could have faced death! I might have just left those people from the plane and never saw them again. Maybe I could have offended them so much they bad-mouthed me to all their friends and co-workers. I am an extremely cautious person. I only take calculated risks. The risk did not outweigh the reward in this situation! I could have brought a believer to God or maybe I could have just planted a seed, either way, I didn't live on the edge for my Lord. I placed my discomfort above their salvation."

Tears streamed down my face during my entire speech. I felt as though I was making the most public confession of my life. My "Christian Life Well-Lived" was getting a tarnished reputation. It definitely was not the presentation I was expecting to give and it most definitely was not the presentation the audience was expecting to hear! Some cried with me. Some walked away emotionless. Others confronted me sternly. All I can say is that the Lord was working on me. The Lord was calling me to take a stand, and he was calling me to do something outside of my comfort zone.

My story of conviction does not simply focus on my lack of public witnessing or my lack of commitment to reading my Bible. It is about my direct disobedience to what I know the Lord was calling me to do. Conviction comes in many forms. Sometimes, we blatantly deny it, pretending we don't see, feel, or hear. Conviction is pushing you to admit something's wrong. It's that gentle tug or callous thrashing on your heart, leading you to correct your path in life. Listen to it.

We are only human, prone to making mistakes. Even though we may know the difference between right and wrong, our judgment and decision-making skills can sometimes be misguided, and the enemy may deceive us. In moments where we have failed to answer conviction and make the right choices, we must learn to love the correction that follows. We must view it as an opportunity for growth and not cower in what feels like failure. We are all, by nature, sinful. However, our mistakes do not define us. They are not our identity. They do not determine our self-worth. How we respond and react to them does. Learn to turn your mistakes into masterpieces. Answer the call of conviction.

"My child, don't reject the Lord's discipline, and don't be upset when he corrects you. For the Lord corrects those he loves, just as a father corrects a child in whom he delights." (Proverbs 3:11-12)

"An open rebuke is better than hidden love! Wounds from a sincere friend are better than many kisses from an enemy." (Proverbs 27:5-6)

"If you listen to constructive criticism, you will be at home among the wise. If you reject discipline, you only harm yourself; but if you listen to correction, you grow in understanding." (Proverbs 15:31-32)

"People who accept discipline are on the pathway to life, but those who ignore correction will go astray." (Proverbs 10:17)

Question & Answer

Listening to Conviction

1. Describe a time when you felt convicted.

2. When you were faced with conviction, did your behavior change?

3. Does discipline make you feel more spiritually connected or disconnected? Why?

4. Do you own your mistakes, or try to place blame elsewhere?

5. How do you separate your need for correction from your self-worth?

6. What is the Lord calling you to correct in your life?

7. How do you plan to make a change?

Prayer

Lord, teach me to love discipline. Teach me to embrace the opportunity for positive change. Where I need attention, convict me, Lord. Show me the areas of my life that are not glorifying you. Help me to distinguish between right and wrong, and no matter the difficulty, to always do what is right. Grant me the discernment to use good judgment as it pertains to my home, my career, and my relationships. When correction presents itself, help me to accept it with an open heart and open mind, making the necessary changes and doing so with joy. Lord, remind me that my value is not based on my mistakes and that your precious blood covers all of my sin. Praise you, God, for your abundant grace. Amen.

Personal Prayer Direction

What are you grateful for this week?

Who are you praying for this week?

Merely Moving Shadows

CHAPTER EIGHT

PURPOSE

Living with a purpose. Doing something meaningful. Making the most out of our time here on Earth. The daily grind tests us every day and makes us question whether or not we are living out our purpose. Get up. Get ready. Work. Come home. Go to bed. Repeat. Between the coffee breaks and commutes, where and how do we establish and fulfill our purpose?

We've all heard the story of creation. After God created the heavens and the earth and all things in and of it, he created man and woman to care for it. We are a significant part of the Lord's grand design; it is clearly stated in his word. So, if we believe the Lord made us **on** purpose, shouldn't we also believe he made us **for** a purpose?

I began my work as a public speaker in the summer of 2008. Becoming Miss America 2009 made it my full-time job and for years I toured regularly, speaking on agriculture, service, goal-setting, and faith. No matter how many times I've given a keynote address, no matter the size of the audience, I still get butterflies, and I still question my preparedness or my qualifications to even be there.

On one special occasion, I was brought in to speak to a high school. I remember feeling anxious and ill-prepared prior to my presentation. I always take a moment to pray before each engagement, and as I stepped on to the floor of the gymnasium, I whispered, (as I do before every presentation). *"Lord, I know that you have already put your words in my mouth. Use me as a catalyst for your will."*

After I finished my address to the student body, I felt disappointed. I did not do my best. I was not eloquent. I offered no grand idea. I even felt as though I had a difficult time connecting with my audience. Nevertheless, I stayed to speak to a number of students before heading back home. One particular student walked over and handed me a bracelet, saying that she wanted me to have it. It was a cute, baby blue, silicone band with several colorful beads strung on it, spelling out the name *Morgan*. Noticing that it was handmade, I immediately handed it back to her, letting her know that it seemed too personal and too special to keep. She insisted that I take it, and then told me her story. She was Morgan, and prior to that day's convocation, she had been contemplating suicide. But after hearing my presentation, she knew that taking her own life wasn't the path for her. I stood frozen. I felt guilty, knowing I had not offered my best that day. I was completely undeserving of the precious gifts of her bracelet and of her words. I reached out and enveloped her in a full embrace, offering all the gratitude and encouragement I could. The experience was shocking, and it was humbling. On my drive home, as I reflected on the day, I couldn't remember a single detail of my speech. All I could see was Morgan.

I want to be very clear about one thing: nothing that I said or did that day saved Morgan. It was Jesus. It was all him. But I believe he used me to reach Morgan. I don't know what specific words spoke to her that day, but they came from him! The Lord carefully crafted a message to reach just her. She was suffocating in the darkness that enveloped her, and it was his light that overthrew that darkness. I felt a tremendous sense of pride in my Savior! He can work miracles even in the darkest of places. I also felt a tremendous sense of purpose: I'd asked him to use me that day, and he **did.**

Even when I didn't know, feel, or believe I was doing anything remotely spectacular, or even anything average, God was still using me for a purpose.

God is working in every moment. He is moving mountains. When we offer our lives up to his work, we can witness miracles.

If you are anything like me, you have asked yourself a few questions.

What is my purpose?

Stop. Change the sentence. It's not your purpose. It's *his purpose for you.* And fulfilling his purpose is fulfilling his promise. In essence, we all have the same purpose: extending his kingdom; but we will all fulfill his purpose differently through our jobs, our relationships, and how we choose to spend our time.

How do I know I have achieved his purpose?

It's easy to feel fulfilled when we feel appreciated, when we see a visible impact, change, or even slight alteration, or when we feel humbled or can take pride in a particular outcome. But don't seek the outcome, and don't seek the appreciation. Seek the Savior.

In seemingly insignificant moments, we can be making the greatest impact if we just ask for him to use us.

"So, my dear brothers and sisters, be strong and immovable. Always work enthusiastically for the Lord, for you know that nothing you do for the Lord is ever useless." (1 Corinthians 15:58)

"The one who plants and the one who waters work together with the same purpose. And both will be rewarded for their own hard work." (1 Corinthians 3:8)

"And we know that God causes everything to work together for the good of those who love God and are called according to his purpose for them." (Romans 8:28)

"I tell you the truth, until heaven and earth disappear, not even the smallest detail of God's law will disappear until its purpose is achieved. (Matthew 5:18)

Question & Answer

Living God's Purpose

1. What is something you do that makes you feel great?

2. Who inspires you most? What qualities in them inspire you?

3. What are your deepest values?

4. Picture yourself at the end of your life. Looking back, what are you most proud of?

5. What is your personal mission statement?

Prayer

Lord God Most High, please use me for your purpose. Send me out to touch the lives of others and bring them back to you. As you offered your life as a sacrifice to save mine, I too, give you my life as an offering to save others. Use me for your will. When I fear I may fail, remind me that you will be my words. You will be my heart. You will be my light, and you will be my success. Amen.

Personal Prayer Direction

What are you grateful for this week?

Who are you praying for this week?

CHAPTER NINE

SUCCESS

I love setting goals. There's not a day that goes by that I don't set at least one. My goal for the day could be as simple as being on time, or as large as a major career shift. With many daily goals, success can easily be measured. With other goals, the measure of success is not definitive; rather, success is defined by general movement toward an end result. It's the journey and the small victories—even with the stumbles and falls we experience along the way—that teach us the most. Even more valuable than the dream coming to fruition, the journey of *chasing* our dreams develops us personally, professionally, and spiritually, inspires us to create new dreams, and builds confidence and self-awareness.

But what happens once we have achieved success? What about when we reach our goals? How do we move past a dream to which we've dedicated so much? What happens when we fail? How about when we feel inadequate or become defeated?

Three years after becoming Miss America, I was invited back to the national pageant as a judge. I was six weeks pregnant with my first child, a few months away from my college graduation, and I was desperately seeking the answer to the question of where God was placing me in my next season of life.

Judging the pageant was an incredible experience. Each year's pageant is like a huge, extended-family reunion. During a brief conversation with a friend in attendance, I mentioned my desire to seek out new career opportunities, but admitted that I had no idea what that looked like. I valued staying at home to raise my children, but I still loved to work. I wanted to find a balance where I could do both. At that point in my career, I was traveling a lot, so I was considering something that would keep me closer to home. My friend was adamant that I have a conversation with their agent. My degree is in television broadcasting, and since I have years of experience within the field, I always thought at some point I would circle back to it if the right job came around. My friend was insistent that this agent would hold the key to my future success in broadcasting, so although I was not actively seeking a television job opportunity *or* an agent, I obliged and set up a phone conference.

I have never felt more belittled, embarrassed, or worthless than after that phone call. I felt as though I did not have enough value to take up this individual's precious time. At one point, the agent sarcastically and aggressively asked, "So what have you done since Miss America?" As I started to describe my speaking tour, completing my college degree, and working in the corporate sector, she interrupted once more with, "But, **what** have you done outside of Miss America that people would care about?" At the close of our conversation, I was informed that not only was I not "big" enough for her to take on as a client, but I did not "have anything" that any of her colleagues would be looking for, either. It was brutal.

It took me a few weeks, if not months, to recover from that phone call. I could not get that conversation out of my head and the feelings of inadequacy out of my heart. I started to believe that the world would never care about me as a "former." My thoughts were weaving a dangerous trap as I wrapped my identity in the words of this woman. I started to think that the older I would get; the further I would find myself from what I had accomplished; therefore, becoming less valuable along the way. I had defined my life's journey by my past success.

The devil seeks to steal, kill, and destroy. If he can't destroy us, he will divide us. If he can't divide us, then he will distract us. The devil had accomplished the latter two of the three in me, and was edging close to my destruction. He had divided me by challenging my value through my successes and making me doubt my ability to produce more success after Miss America. I withdrew from others, believing I wasn't good enough. He had distracted me, making me believe that my past success was all I would ever amount to, the best of my years were behind me, and I had nothing more for which to aspire. My future dreams had diminished in the blink of an eye. I continued down the path to total destruction as I tried to convince myself that I'd never amount to anything more than a has-been—and that I was okay with that. All of this torment resulted from a three-minute phone call with a person I had never met, who knew nothing about me and would make no effort to do so.

Becoming Miss America fulfilled a life-long dream I'd had since the age of three, and it's an accomplishment that I am tremendously proud of and humbled by—but I'm not done dreaming. Wearing that crown did not define my life's success or my life's journey. Has it made a huge impact? Yes. Would I be where I am today if I hadn't become Miss America? No. But, it wasn't the crown, the title, or the prestige that made me who I am today; it was the character building, the lessons I learned, and the values and behavioral traits I developed along the way. If anything, becoming Miss America taught me not to settle. It taught me to keep dreaming, keep doing, keep learning, and keep growing.

As we grow and our dreams evolve, we must be able to identify the source of our desire for meeting our goals. If we are confident that a dream has been put on our heart by him, then we must pursue that dream with the intent of using it for his glory and his kingdom. If the pursuit doesn't bring him glory, and if we have to compromise morally and spiritually to pursue it, then it isn't from him. Once we start pursuing our new dreams, we must let the Lord entirely reshape our metrics for measuring success, because worldly success and Kingdom success are not the same. Francis Chan wrote, "Our greatest fear should not be of failure, but of succeeding at things in life that don't really matter!" Let's set our minds and our hearts to things that truly matter.

Do you ever feel like your best days are behind you? Do you ever feel like you've lived your best life and now you have to settle for whatever's left? Do you feel like your past mistakes have left you incapable of becoming something more? If you answered no to any of these, Praise God! But if you answered yes, the Lord wants you to know that **you are not what you do**, and **you are not what you have done.**

Chan, Francis. *Crazy love: Overwhelmed by a relentless God*. David C Cook, 2013.

Your successes do not define your value, and neither do your mistakes, your failures, or your insecurities.

Your title, your position, and your qualifications do not define your abilities.

Your past experiences, your obstacles, and your failures, or even your successes, do not define your future.

Who you are and what you choose today will impact where you go next. But remember, your destination is not definitive of your journey. Everything of this world is fleeting. **Everything.**

The next time the devil attempts to make you question your value through someone or something, know that Jesus has deemed you **invaluable**!

It matters not who or what you are, but rather **whose** you are. And it matters not where you are going, as long as you know that heaven is your ultimate destination.

Jesus gave his life for you. He took your place. Christ has become your new identity. When we accept Christ, we take on his name as our own: Christian. Therefore, we must strive to be more like him in the ways we act, react, and love. We must always try to be more like Jesus, seeking spiritual success.

No matter our lot in life. No matter our struggles. No matter our pinnacle of success or depth of our failure: we are his, and he has already claimed the greatest victory!

"Study this Book of Instruction continually. Meditate on it day and night so you will be sure to obey everything written in it. Only then will you prosper and succeed in all you do." (Joshua 1:8)

"'For see, today I have made you strong like a fortified city that cannot be captured, like an iron pillar or a bronze wall. You will stand against the whole land – the kings, officials, priests, and people of Judah. They will fight you, but they will fail. For I am with you, and I will take care of you. I, the Lord, have spoken!'" (Jeremiah 1:18-19)

"Work willingly at whatever you do, as though you were working for the Lord rather than for people. Remember that the Lord will give you an inheritance as your reward, and that the Master you are serving is Christ." (Colossians 3:23-24)

"The Lord says, 'I will guide you along the best pathway for your life. I will advise you and watch over you.'" (Psalms 32:8)

Question & Answer

Sorting through Success

1. Describe a time in your life that you felt you reached the pinnacle of success.

If you believe you have not yet reached that pinnacle, what do you imagine it would look like?

2. What is something you accomplished, or believe you could accomplish, by reaching the pinnacle from the first question, other than the tangible outcome of your success?

3. What is your measure of success? How do you know you've succeeded?

4. Do you believe success equals happiness?

5. Do you believe failure equals sadness or even depression?

6. Have there been failures that have actually made your life better?

7. How are failure and weakness different?

8. How are success and strength different?

Prayer

Lord, I praise you for my past experiences. You have granted me so many opportunities to learn, to grow, and to dream. Thank you for the beauty of dreams and the ability to seek them. Lord, continue to remind me that my past is not my identity. Be a constant message in my ears that **you** are my identity. You have saved me, you have called me, and you have claimed me as one of your own. You live in me and are a part of me. Let every breath I breathe, every action I take, and every dream I dream be glorifying to you. Amen.

Personal Prayer Direction

What are you grateful for this week?

Who are you praying for this week?

CHAPTER TEN
COMMUNITY

Life change happens in the context of relationships.

Most people assume that moments after the Miss America crown was placed on my head, I was able to walk off the stage and immediately begin my celebration with my family and friends. The reality is that the job starts instantaneously, and the celebrating must wait. After the television cameras stopped rolling, I spent nearly three hours meeting with the press, giving a speech, and greeting sponsors before I was escorted to my new hotel suite, where twenty-five family members and friends waited. For twenty minutes we hugged, we cried, and we celebrated! Shortly after, everyone was asked to leave, and I was left alone, staring blankly at the two suitcases that were filled with my belongings for the next year.

If it hadn't been for a wonderful woman named Debbie, I would have been extremely lost. I don't think I would have slept. I don't think I would have ever taken off the crown or even my evening gown. In the blink of an eye, everything I had come to identify as typical life was launched like a rocket into outer space, and I was left hovering among the stars.

Debbie sat me down and offered words of wisdom that would carry me through the next year. She told me that there would be days I would want to quit. In the moment, I found that really hard to believe. But after traveling 250,000 miles in one year, changing locations every 18-48 hours, and living out of hotels and suitcases and restaurants, life as Miss America would get tiresome. It would be in those moments that the job would be most important. There would always be someone in need of encouragement, a helping hand, or a smiling face—and some days, that someone would be me. I had no idea how impactful that message would be over the next twelve months, and really, for the rest of my life. Debbie told me to take off the crown, place it in its carrying case, and put it off to the side, reassuring me, "There would be enough time to wear that in the days to come." She taught me how to hand-wash my undergarments in the bathroom sink, because that would be my method for washing clothes while on the road for the next year. And then she told me to lie down to get some rest.

The next morning, I woke up and prepared for a meeting with the staff of the organization. My parents joined me for what would be an eye-opening few minutes. The staff spent their time outlining my new normal and asking more about me so that they could map out the groups and organizations with which to connect me for the coming year. I told them that I was a ten-year 4-H member, I grew up on a dairy farm, I love all things music, and that I was a very strong

Christian. At that moment, the air felt like it was sucked out of the room. I sat confused at the silence, and finally, one of the women spoke up to say that while everyone in the room shared my faith, Miss America is to remain representative of all beliefs, religions, and backgrounds. Because of this, I was not to speak about Jesus or my faith unless I was asked. Although I understood the reasons behind this, I knew that it would be an incredible challenge.

Jesus met that challenge.

During my year of service, I came in to contact with hundreds of thousands of people. And nearly everywhere I went, someone asked me about Jesus. On a daily basis, no matter the engagement, someone prompted a question about my faith, giving me a chance to witness fully within the communicated guidelines of the organization. (Although I believe it's even okay to break the rules for Jesus every once and awhile!)

In every moment, the Lord was working to create opportunities for him. On the hard days, it didn't matter how tired, how defeated, or how discouraged I had become, because I had an important job to do. And, as the famous saying goes, "80% of success is showing up." The Holy Spirit was stirring in the hearts of those people who started the conversation with me about my faith as I served as Miss America. Each and every opportunity was a chance to make a difference in someone's life by introducing Jesus. I had no power or control over any of it, but my prayer was and continues to be that he uses me. Jesus works through relationships to reach his lost sheep. If you'll just show up, he will do the rest.

Whether I was given twenty seconds, twenty minutes, or two hours with someone, the relationships were what mattered. During those times when I had enough energy to run a marathon, as well as those times that I wanted to curl up in bed and shut out the world, the relationships were what mattered.

How can we make an impact for Jesus? How do we live our full potential? How can we reach our goals, overcome obstacles, celebrate the triumphs, and navigate the rough waters of grief and loss? How do we ensure that we will not travel through life as merely moving shadows? The answer is *community*.

Living in relationship is learning how to love sacrificially. Jesus is the epitome of sacrificial love. If we want to make the most out of life, we must strive to live like Jesus; we must strive to love others the way he did.

If you take nothing else away from this study, take this: **don't do life alone**. If you are hurting, lost, or broken, don't do it alone. If you are grieving, hopeless, or afraid, don't do it alone. And if you are happy, joyful, or at peace, don't do it alone! Make an investment in others. Take the time to share your story, your kindness, and your love—and open yourself up to receive the same from another. Jesus can bring resolution, peace, hope, and joy to your life through the people with whom you surround yourself. Your community is made up of those with whom you have committed to do life; whether you're worshipping together, praying for one another, mourning or rejoicing with one another, or encouraging one another in the faith. Community is intentional and it is ongoing.

Here are a few disclaimers: Find the right person to walk through life with. Two broken people don't make a whole person. If you are feeling empty, do some soul searching to identify the emptiness. I guarantee your fulfillment can be met in Christ. A God-shaped hole in your heart can only be filled with God. No person can replace God, and no person will ever complete you or offer you true fulfillment. But a friend can extend support. A confidant can offer accountability. A mentor can impart wisdom.

One of my closest friends once said of her husband, "We don't work well together because we are perfect for each other. We work well together because we point each other to the One who is." Every relationship must have God at the core to be as successful as possible.

There is a relatively common illustration in faith-based literature that presents relationships as crafted in the form of a triangle. The triangle is the strongest shape in architecture and it beautifully identifies the structure of a Godly relationship. The bottom two points are assigned to yourself and a friend, spouse, mentor, or other person in your community. The top point represents God. As you travel up the sides of the triangle, you continue to draw nearer to God. As you draw nearer to God, you grow closer to each other. Healthy, strong relationships are those that are built on a Godly foundation.

The Lord intended for us to live in Godly relationship, as illustrated in Matthew 18:20: "For where two or more of you are gathered, there I will be." Create your sphere of relationships so that you may gather together in the presence of the Lord. Join a small group, volunteer, tutor, work with children's mentoring programs, participate in a local club, or attend community functions. Find a way to connect with people, and then start a conversation.

When you are hesitant about starting the conversation, find encouragement through God's word. The first chapter of Jeremiah tells the story of when the Lord called Jeremiah to be a prophet. Jeremiah's immediate response to the call was resistance, as he feared his inadequacies. But the Lord promised Jeremiah success. Here's Jeremiah's story:

"The Lord gave me this message: 'I knew you before I formed you in your mother's womb. Before you were born I set you apart and appointed you as my prophet to the nations.' 'O Sovereign Lord,' I said, 'I can't speak for you! I'm too young!' The Lord replied, 'Don't say, 'I'm too young,' for you must go wherever I send you and say whatever I tell you. And don't be afraid of the people, for I will be with you and will protect you. I, the Lord, have spoken!' Then the Lord reached out and touched my mouth and said, 'Look, I have put my words in your mouth! Today I appoint you to stand up against nations and kingdoms. Some you must uproot and tear down, destroy and overthrow. Others you must build up and plant.'

'For see, today I have made you strong like a fortified city that cannot be captured, like an iron pillar or a bronze wall. You will stand against the whole land— the kings, officials, priests, and people of Judah. They will fight you, but they will fail. For I am with you, and I will take care of you. I, the Lord, have spoken!'" (Jeremiah 1:4-10,18-19)

The Lord has already put his words into your mouth. He has promised you success.

The late, great Erma Bombeck once wrote, "When I stand before God at the end of my days, I would hope to have not one bit of talent left, and I could say, 'I used everything you gave me.'" Use everything he's given you until you have nothing left to give. Let the Lord work through you. Be a constant flow of love and information in relationship, and do it all in the name of the Lord.

Trust in God's timing, find the beauty in your journey, choose to forgive, stand firm with the Lord's strength, deal with your discontentment, live fearlessly, listen to conviction, seek the Lord's purpose, strive for success in Christ, and pursue relationships to love others well.

God's blessings on your journey.

"A friend is always loyal, and a brother is born to help in time of need." (Proverbs 17:17)

"Let us think of ways to motivate one another to acts of love and good works. And let us not neglect our meeting together, as some people do. But encourage one another, especially now that the day of his return is drawing near." (Hebrews 10:24-25)

"Above all, clothe yourselves with love, which binds us all together in perfect harmony. And let the peace that comes from Christ rule in your hearts. For as members of one body you are called to live in peace. And always be thankful." (Colossians 3:14-15)

"They worshiped together at the Temple each day, met in homes for the Lord's Supper, and shared their meals with great joy and generosity –all the while praising God and enjoying the goodwill of all the people. And each day the Lord added to their fellowship those who were being saved." (Acts 2:46-47)

Question & Answer

Living in Relationship

1. Are you positively impacted by those with whom you spend the most time?

2. Are you positively impacting the lives of those with whom you spend the most time?

3. What are the most important qualities your friends possess?

4. How do you show others that you love them?

5. Who in your life has influenced you most?

6. Who have you had the most influence on?

Prayer

Lord, thank you for the blessing of relationship. Thank you for the ability to be in a position of influence in others' lives. Be a constant reminder on my heart to love others well. Help me slow down so that I may invest more time in others. Help me to be a good listener so that I may truly hear the needs of those around me. Help me be a positive influence for everyone I come in contact with. Thank you for opportunities of mentorship. Thank you for every opportunity to be your light. Amen.

Personal Prayer Direction

What are you grateful for this week?

Who are you praying for this week?

DEVOTIONAL CHALLENGE

As you reflect on the time you devoted to this study, I pray that the Lord speaks to you in the areas of your life that can be used to glorify him. It is by design that the final chapter of this devotional is about relationships and living in community.

Over the next few days, really focus on living intentionally with those around you. When the Lord puts the name of someone on your heart, send a quick text or email, make a quick phone call, or reach out to them on social media. A simple note to let someone know that you're thinking of them can make a huge impact, and can allow you to be a light in their life at just the right time.

Take it a step further and set aside some time to write a love letter to your family and friends. Share with them why you love them, what makes them special, and how grateful you are to have them in your life. Either drop the letters in the mail or hand-deliver them. Reconnect with those around you. Take the time to tell them how much they mean to you. It will bring so much joy, light, and encouragement to your life!

AUTHOR'S NOTE

Stay in touch with Katie by using
#merelymovingshadows
on social media once you complete the study.

ACKNOWLEDGMENTS

A very special **THANK YOU** to these dear friends for their contributions, love, and encouragement:

Craig Miller, Kim Tabor, Brian Irk, Caryn Goo, Erica Hightower, Chad Hightower & Hightower Graphics (*Graphics Support & Printer*), Sheila Dolan, Corey Diehl, Jen Gavin, Sierra Vogt (*Editor*), Ellie Rose, Sonja Castelluccio, Lynn Wheeler, Pastor Ralph Blomenberg, Julie Earlewine, Michael Nash, Heather Florido, Eric Stam, Heidi Lawrence, David Lawrence, Carlos Florido, Keith Stam, Tracy Stam, Misty Brown, Carolyn Nelson, Jackie Watson, and Jennifer Driscoll (*Photographer*).

And many more for your inspiration.
I love you all.

Merely Moving Shadows